ISBN 978-0-266-05422-1
PIBN 11037528

CARICATURES PERTAINING TO THE CIVIL WAR:
REPRODUCED FROM A PRIVATE COLLECTION OF ORIGI-
NALS DESIGNED FOR CURRIER & IVES, NEW YORK, AND
PUBLISHED BY THEM IN SHEETS FROM 1856 TO 1872.
AND NOW FOR THE FIRST TIME PUBLISHED IN BOOK
FORM.

WRIGHT & SWASEY,
(WRIGHT GRAVURE CO.)
NEW YORK.
1892.

CARICATURES *PERTAINING TO THE CIVIL WAR: REPRODUCED FROM A PRIVATE COLLECTION OF ORIGI- NALS DESIGNED FOR CURRIER & IVES, NEW YORK, AND PUBLISHED BY THEM IN SHEETS FROM 1856 TO 1872, AND NOW FOR THE FIRST TIME PUBLISHED IN BOOK FORM.*

WRIGHT & SWASEY,
(WRIGHT GRAVURE CO.)
NEW YORK.
1892.

THE DEMOCRATIC PLATFORM.

THE "MUSTANG" TEAM

THE RIGHT MAN FOR THE RIGHT PLACE.

THE GREAT REPUBLICAN REFORM PARTY,
Calling on their Candidate.

THE GREAT REPUBLICAN REFORM PARTY,
Calling on their Candidate.

THE GREAT MATCH AT BALTIMORE.
BETWEEN THE "ILLINOIS BANTAM", AND THE "OLD COCK" OF THE WHITE HOUSE.

THE GREAT MATCH AT BALTIMORE,
BETWEEN THE "ILLINOIS BANTAM," AND THE "OLD COCK" OF THE WHITE HOUSE.

"TAKING THE STUMP" OR STEPHEN IN SEARCH OF HIS MOTHER.

"TAKING THE STUMP" OR STEPHEN IN SEARCH OF HIS MOTHER.

STEPHEN FINDING "HIS MOTHER".

STEPHEN FINDING "HIS MOTHER".

STORMING THE CASTLE
"OLD ABE" ON GUARD.

STORMING THE CASTLE
"OLD ABE" ON GUARD.

THE NATIONAL GAME. THREE "OUTS" AND ONE "RUN".
ABRAHAM WINNING THE BALL.

THE NATIONAL GAME. THREE "OUTS" AND ONE "RUN".
ABRAHAM WINNING THE BALL.

THE FOLLY OF SECESSION.

THE FOLLY OF SECESSION.

SOUTH CAROLINA'S "ULTIMATUM".

SOUTH CAROLINA'S "ULTIMATUM".

UNCLE SAM MAKING NEW ARRANGEMENTS.

UNCLE SAM MAKING NEW ARRANGEMENTS.

PROGRESSIVE DEMOCRACY—PROSPECT OF A SMASH UP.

POLITICAL "BLONDINS" CROSSING SALT RIVER.

POLITICAL "BLONDINS" CROSSING SALT RIVER.

THE RAIL CANDIDATE.

THE RAIL CANDIDATE.

"THE NIGGER" IN THE WOODPILE.

"THE NIGGER" IN THE WOODPILE.

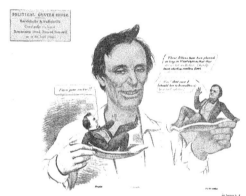

HONEST ABE TAKING THEM ON THE HALF SHELL..

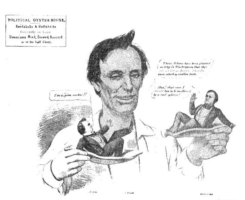

HONEST ABE TAKING THEM ON THE HALF SHELL.

THE GREAT EXHIBITION OF 1860.

THE GREAT EXHIBITION OF 1860.

"THE IRREPRESSIBLE CONFLICT".
OR THE REPUBLICAN BARGE IN DANGER.

"THE IRREPRESSIBLE CONFLICT".
OR THE REPUBLICAN BARGE IN DANGER.

"THE IMPENDING CRISIS"_OR CAUGHT IN THE ACT.

"THE IMPENDING CRISIS"—OR CAUGHT IN THE ACT.

LETTING THE CAT OUT OF THE BAG!!

LETTING **THE CAT** OUT OF THE **BAG!!**

AN HEIR TO THE THRONE,
OR THE NEXT REPUBLICAN CANDIDATE

AN HEIR TO THE THRONE,
OR THE NEXT REPUBLICAN CANDIDATE

THE REPUBLICAN PARTY GOING TO THE RIGHT HOUSE.

THE REPUBLICAN PARTY GOING TO THE RIGHT HOUSE.

THE POLITICAL GYMNASIUM.

THE **POLITICAL GYMNASIUM.**

THE "SECESSION MOVEMENT".

THE "SECESSION MOVEMENT".

THE OLD GENERAL READY FOR A "MOVEMENT".

THE OLD GENERAL READY FOR A "MOVEMENT".

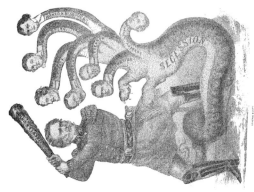

THE HERCULES OF THE UNION,
SLAYING THE GREAT DRAGON OF SECESSION.

THE HERCULES OF THE UNION,

SLAYING THE GREAT DRAGON OF SECESSION.

THE FOX WITHOUT A TAIL.

A cunning fox having lost his tail in a trap, to save himself from ridicule called a meeting of the other foxes and stated to them that having found his tail a great inconvenience he had cut it off and advised them all to do the same, he would in save...

THE FOX WITHOUT A TAIL.

A cunning fox having lost his tail in a trap to save himself from ridicule, called a assemblage of the other foxes and tried whom that having found his tail a great convenience to kind art it off and make them all to do the same, the most a men where.

THE DIS-UNITED STATES.
OR THE SOUTHERN CONFEDERACY

THE DIS-UNITED STATES.
OR THE SOUTHERN CONFEDERACY

SOUTHERN "VOLUNTEERS".

SOUTHERN "VOLUNTEERS".

WHY DON'T YOU TAKE IT?

WHY DON'T YOU TAKE IT!

CAVING IN, OR A REBEL "DEEPLY HUMILIATED".

CAVING IN, OR A REBEL "DEEPLY HUMILIATED".

JOHN BULL MAKES A DISCOVERY.

JOHN BULL MAKES A DISCOVERY.

THE BLOCKADE ON THE "CONNECTICUT PLAN".

Respectfully dedicated to the Secretary of the Navy.

THE·BLOCKADE ON THE "CONNECTICUT PLAN".

THE BATTLE OF BOONEVILLE, OR THE GREAT MISSOURI 'LYON' HUNT.

THE BATTLE OF BOONEVILLE. OR THE GREAT MISSOURI "LYON" HUNT.

THE VOLUNTARY MANNER IN WHICH SOME OF THE SOUTHERN VOLUNTEERS ENLIST.

THE VOLUNTARY MANNER IN WHICH SOME OF THE SOUTHERN VOLUNTEERS ENLIST.

HEADS OF THE DEMOCRACY.

HEADS OF THE DEMOCRACY.

DESPERATE PEACE MAN.

DESPERATE PEACE MAN.

THE TRUE ISSUE OR "THATS WHATS THE MATTER".

THE TRUE ISSUE OR "THATS WHATS THE MATTER".

THE GUNBOAT CANDIDATE
AT THE BATTLE OF MALVERN HILL.

THE GUNBOAT CANDIDATE

AT THE BATTLE OF MALVERN HILL.

A LITTLE GAME OF BAGATELLE, BETWEEN OLD ABE THE RAIL SPLITTER & LITTLE MAC THE GUNBOAT GENERAL.

A LITTLE GAME OF BAGATELLE, BETWEEN OLD ABE THE RAIL SPLITTER & LITTLE MAC THE GUNBOAT GENERAL.

RUNNING THE "MACHINE".

SD - #0031 - 130625 - C0 - 229/152/6 - PB - 9780266054221 - Gloss Lamination